Sue Fox

# Hermit Crabs

Everything About Anatomy, Ecology, Purchasing, Feeding, Housing, Behavior, and Illness

Filled with Full-color Photographs

# 2 CONTENTS

## What Are Crustaceans?

Crabs, shrimps, prawns, lobsters, barnacles, and woodlice (sowbugs and pillbugs) are all crustaceans. Approximately 25,000 species of crustaceans are found throughout the world. Crustaceans belong to the phylum arthropoda, which contains two out of every three living organisms. Arthropods have jointed limbs and a hard outer covering over their bodies, called the exoskeleton. Insects, spiders, scorpions, millipedes, and centipedes are also arthropods. Found almost everywhere on earth, arthropods are the most successful phylum of animals ever to live. They are far more abundant than vertebrates, such as fish, mammals, and birds.

### Distinguishing Features

Crustaceans are distinguished from other arthropods by two sets of antennae instead of only one. Their numerous jointed appendages are used for a variety of purposes, including walking, eating, and sensory perception. Like the more well-known insects, crustaceans also develop from larvae. While insects and spiders are mostly found on land, crustaceans are found mainly in oceans, lakes, and ponds. Two exceptions are sowbugs and pillbugs, which are small, land-dwelling crustaceans familiar to many people.

*There are about 800 species of hermit crabs; only 12 are semiterrestrial, the rest are marine.*

**Decapoda.** Crabs, lobsters, and shrimps are crustaceans that belong to the scientific order decapoda. The name decapoda means "ten feet" and all the animals in this order have five pairs of legs, thus ten feet. Most decapods live in the ocean, but some, such as crayfish, live in freshwater, and others, such as the tropical land hermit crabs, live mainly on land.

## Environment

Hermit crabs are found from the polar to tropical seas. They live in deep ocean canyons, along the ocean shore, and several miles inland from the sea. Of the approximately 6,000 species of crabs known to science, about 800 are hermit crabs. Only 12 of these species are semiterrestrial; the rest are marine. Hermit crabs might have spread to so many different environments because of their unique lifestyle, which includes a protective snail shell that functions as a mobile home.

The hot tropical sun is dangerous to land hermit crabs and can dehydrate them. The crabs are most active at night, when the evaporative water loss is likely to be lower. During the day, most land hermit crabs hide in shallow burrows, niches among tree roots and branches, or beneath leaves, rocks, and fallen branches. Favorable places are sometimes inhabited by dozens of crabs sleeping in compact clusters. When it is very humid or has just rained, crabs occasionally wander about during the day.

In the wild, hermit crabs regularly interact with one another. Because the crabs are attracted to the same sources of food and shelter, they are often found together. When a crab sees other crabs feeding, it hurries over to join the others. At night they are often seen in large groups feeding along the ocean shore. It is common for hermit crabs to climb over each other rather than walk around a group of fellow crabs.

## True Crabs vs. Hermit Crabs

True crabs, which scientists place in the order brachyura, have a short abdomen that is folded up under the large calcified shell on their backs. If you have ever eaten whole crab for dinner, you might have noticed this. Although hermit crabs have features in common with their crab relatives, they are not considered true crabs. Scientists place them in their own order: anomuran crabs. Other members of this order are mole crabs and robber crabs.

*A land hermit crab crawls out of a hollow log.*

Unlike a true crab, a hermit crab's long abdomen sticks out at the rear of its body. Because the abdomen does not have a hard covering of chitin, a hermit crab must conceal its uncalcified abdomen within an empty snail shell of the appropriate size. A hermit crab's abdomen typically curves to the right. The shells of most marine snails have spirals that coil to the right; thus, a hermit crab can easily fit into these shells.

Most species of hermit crab are adapted to live in empty snail shells and are mobile. However, some species tuck their abdomens into shelters that cannot move around. Such unconventional homes include pieces of bamboo, tubes produced by marine worms, and cavities in corals, sponges, or stones. Many of the species inhabiting attached tubes or cavities can no longer move about and rarely, if ever, leave their housing.

*Pet hermit crabs are members of the genus* Coenobita.

## Taxonomy

To learn more about your hermit crab, it is helpful to have a brief understanding of taxonomy, the system that scientists use to classify living organisms into hierarchical groups.

### Scientific Names

Scientific names are the means by which scientists from all over the world refer to the same species of animal. The reason that scientists and serious hobbyists use scientific names is that an animal can have several different common names. An animal's common name can vary by region and can even be the same as another animal's common name. For example, the land hermit crab usually sold as a pet is known by several names including tree crab and purple claw crab. In parts of the crab's native island habitat (the Netherlands Antilles), the people call it "soldaatje" or little soldier. However, the crab's scientific name, *Coenobita clypeata,* is always the same. The common name tree crab can also refer to any other species of land hermit crab. The only way to know for certain which species you are talking about is by the scientific name.

**A species name** is made of two parts, the genus and the species epithet. The first letter of the genus name is always capitalized. If the genus was previously written in full, it can also be denoted by the first letter followed by a period. The genus and species names are always italicized or underlined.

**Taxonomic categories** are scientists' method for ordering all living things. The taxonomic groups are the following: kingdom, phylum, class, order, family, genus, and species name. (An easy way to remember the order of the taxonomic groups is: King Philip came over for grape sherbet.) A species is the basic unit of

*Unlike hermit crabs, true crabs tuck their hard abdomen under the shell on their backs.*

## Hermit Crab Classification

Kingdom: Animalia
Phylum: Arthropoda
Subphylum: Mandibulata
Class: Crustacea
Order: Decapoda
Family: Coenobitidae
Genus: Coenobita
Species: Clypeatus

*Scientific names are used to identify species.*

classification. Genera (singular is genus) are groups of species that share a common ancestor. Genera are grouped into families, families into orders, and so forth. In addition, these groups can be subdivided into a number of less important ones, such as subphylum.

Scientific classification can seem complex, boring, and unnecessary for a pet owner. However, this system is useful to you. If you go to a library and look up information on your pet, you are more likely to find your crab listed by species, genus, or family than by a common name.

## The Family Coenobitidae

Crabs in the family Coenobitidae are adapted to terrestrial environments. Coenobitidae contains only two genera, *Birgus* and *Coenobita.* The genus *Birgus* contains only one species, *Birgus latro,* the robber or coconut crab. Found in the jungles of Pacific and Indian Ocean islands, this crab is the largest living land arthropod. Robber crabs grow to an enormous size. Some of the largest known specimens weigh almost 10 pounds (4.5 kg) and their legs span more than 3 feet (1 m)!

Robber crabs can be found at elevations of several hundred feet and locations several miles away from the ocean. The omnivorous crab got its name because it was erroneously credited with climbing coconut palms, breaking off the nuts, and using its claws to crack open the coconuts to eat. When it is small, the robber crab uses a shell to protect its soft abdomen. After about two years, its abdomen hardens and the crab lives without a shell.

*A wild purple claw hermit crab from the Florida Keys.*

## The Genus Coenobita

The land hermit crabs you can buy as pets are members of the genus *Coenobita*. The 11 species that belong to this genus are found in the tropical coastal regions of the world including Africa, the Caribbean, Mexico, Indonesia, the East Indies, and Pakistan. Wherever they live, land hermit crabs are often conspicuous as they wander about at dusk and dawn, sometimes making loud noises as they fall from trees. Unlike most land crabs, which are adapted for walking sideways, land hermit crabs can walk forward. They can also climb trees, which is why they are sometimes called tree crabs. As they climb, they spiral up a branch. It is not uncommon for hermit crabs to lose their grip and drop to the ground during their descent. They are adapted to life on land, but must return to the ocean shore to breed. Compared to most marine hermit crabs, land hermit crabs are less colorful and strikingly marked.

The largest Coenobita species *(Coenobita brevimanus)*, which is found in Tahiti and other locations, can weigh more than a half pound. The smallest species *(Coenobita compressus)* weighs only a little more than one ounce. Some *Coenobita* species live close to the beach, sheltered among tree roots and rocks, never moving more than several hundred feet from the high tide. Other species can be found several miles away from the ocean and at elevations of almost 3,000 feet (914 m). In dense jungles far from the ocean's shore, these crabs burrow into piles of wet, rotting vegetation and stay alive for weeks without drinking any water.

Only two species are sold as pets: *Coenobita clypeatus,* called the purple claw crab, and *Coenobita compressus,* known as the Ecuadorian crab. The purple claw crab is found in the western Atlantic from southern Florida in the United States, the Caribbean Islands, the Bahamas, and the West Indian Islands south to Venezuela. The purple claw crabs often live several miles away from the ocean. As they wander about, they usually avoid marshes and areas with dense grass. The Ecuadorian crabs are found along the West Coast of America from Baja, California, to Chile. The Ecuadorian crabs live on the beach and in the nearby tropical forest. Always found close to the ocean's shore, they roam the shoreline at night, foraging on items washed up by the tide.

# HERMIT CRAB ANATOMY

You will rarely, if ever, be able to see all of your crab, because its posterior half is hidden inside its shell. Nonetheless, it is useful to have an understanding of your pet's anatomy in order to better understand its behavior and how it lives.

## Exoskeleton

The crab's exoskeleton is made from layers of protein and chitin. The exoskeleton, or cuticle, is hardened by calcium carbonate. In some places the cuticle is like thick, hard armor, such as on the crab's claws and back. In other places the cuticle is paper thin and flexible, such as on the joints and appendages. The exoskeleton protects the animal and provides points of attachment for the muscles to move the appendages. It helps impede water loss, although a crab still slowly loses water across its exoskeleton.

## Antennae

These special sense organs help a crab obtain information about its environment. Sometimes called feelers by pet owners, a crab has two pairs of antennae at the front of its head: two are very long and two are short. The long pair are called antennas and the short pair are called antennules.

*A land hermit crab protects its soft abdomen inside its shell.*

Below a crab's eyes are the long antennas. You might notice your crab touching other crabs and the objects in its home with its antennas. The short antennules are located on the outside of a crab's eyes. These are a crab's main chemosensory organs and contain nerve endings sensitive to smell and taste.

A hermit crab's urinary bladders are located at the base of each antennule. You are unlikely to notice your crab's urine because the amount produced is very small. In addition, some of the waste is given off as ammonia gas.

## Eyes

A crab's eyes are located at the end of moveable stalks. Hermit crabs have compound eyes that consist of many tiny lenses. Like other animals with compound eyes, a crab sees images made up of many pieces, similar to a mosaic picture. Although a crab's sense of smell is superior (it can still locate food if its eyes are missing), its vision is important to help the animal find other crabs and food.

## Feeding Appendages

If you are observant, you might notice that your crab has a lot of small appendages around its mouth. Called the maxillipeds, they are composed of three pairs of appendages. A crab uses these specialized appendages like hands. In particular, the third maxillipeds are used to

grasp and tear large pieces of food, to hold food in the crab's mouth as it nibbles, and to groom itself.

## Legs

A crab's five pairs of legs are used for different purposes. At the end of the first pair, called chelipeds, are the crab's powerful claws. A land hermit crab's left claw is larger than its right claw. The left claw is used for climbing and defense. The right claw is normally used for eating and climbing. When a crab retreats inside its shell, it uses the left claw to block the shell opening, like an armored door.

The remaining four pairs of legs are called periopods. A crab's second and third pairs of legs are used for walking. The second pair of legs also function like the antennules, and can be used by the crab to detect food. However, they are not nearly as sensitive.

*A hermit crab uses its two sets of antennae to sense its environment.*

A hermit crab's fourth and fifth pairs of legs are very small and never extend outside its shell. The crab uses these stubby legs to hold itself inside the snail shell and to maneuver the shell while walking. These specialized legs are covered with microscopic scales that help the crab grip its shell.

## Hairs

The long hairs that you see between the joints of your crab's legs, on the maxillipeds, along the inside of some appendages, and near its mouth are called setae. Unlike the hair that grows on your head, setae do not grow from hair follicles. They are actually extensions of the crab's cuticle. When a crab molts its exoskeleton, these "hairs" are also shed as projections of the exoskeleton.

*A land hermit crab has ten legs.*

## Cephalthorax

The hermit crab's head, which contains its mouth, eyes, and antennae, is fused to its thorax and is known as the cephalthorax. The crab's five pairs of legs are attached to the thorax. The portion of the cephalthorax that covers the top of the crab forms a hard protective shield called the carapace. This is the crab's smooth back, which some friendly crabs allow their owners to stroke.

## Gills

A hermit crab's gills are enclosed in the branchial chamber, which functions as a lung. The branchial chamber is located along the

*The enormous coconut crab (Birgus latro) is a type of hermit crab, but only lives in a shell when it is small.*

sides of the thorax, above the crab's legs. A hermit crab breathes through its gills and branchial chamber, which must be kept moist in order to function. If the branchial chamber and gills dry out, the crab will die. Compared to aquatic hermit crabs, land hermit crabs' gills are reduced in size, and if the adult crabs are kept underwater too long, they will drown.

*This hairy marine hermit crab is found in the Hawaiian Islands.*

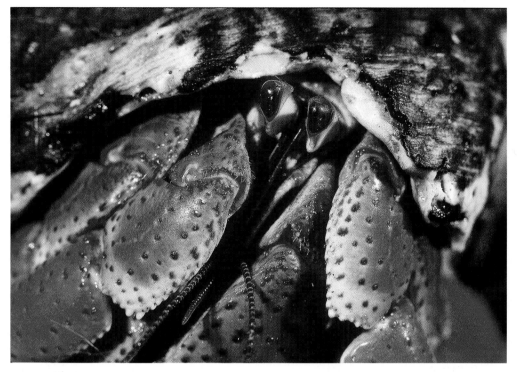

*A close-up view of a land hermit crab.*

## Abdomen

Following the imposing armored appendages and cephalthorax is the vulnerable part of the crab that makes it look less menacing. The soft, cashew-shaped abdomen is not visible; the hermit crab protects it inside the shell. The crab's abdomen contains its digestive and reproductive organs. At the end of the crab's abdomen is the anus. A crab produces small feces that are deposited in its shell. By moving its abdomen about inside its shell, the crab causes the droppings to fall out. Some pet owners refer to a hermit crab's abdomen as its tail.

## Pleopods

The pleopods are small appendages located on the left side of the crab's abdomen. A female crab attaches her eggs to the fine setae on her pleopods using a gluelike substance. Male land hermit crabs also have pleopods, but they are much smaller and not nearly as hairy.

## Uropods

At the tip of a crab's abdomen are small appendages called uropods. Although you will never see them, they perform an important function. The uropods hook onto the spiral of the shell and help the crab to grip its shell.

## Molting

A hermit crab grows by shedding its exoskeleton. For most of the molting process a hermit crab will remain within its protective shell, which usually has a store of water. This water helps protect the crab from drying out while molting. Water is also necessary for the crab to stretch its new exoskeleton before it hardens.

When your crab molts, the exoskeleton on the back of its body begins to split. Sticking its upper body out of its shell, the crab first works its abdomen out of the old covering, then pulls out its front half. It looks like the crab is shimmying as it breaks out of its shed skin. Underneath, there is a new exoskeleton, which is pale pink in color and soft and moist. The hermit crab remains hidden inside its protective shell until the new exoskeleton hardens. During this time, the crab's body swells with water and air, forcing it to grow.

A crab remains in hiding as much as possible while it molts. Many pet hermit crabs bury themselves in the terrarium substrate, and some crabs might remain buried for more than a month. Because of this habit, you are unlikely to observe the entire molting process. A crab that is molting is very vulnerable because it is soft and squishy. Even the crab's usually powerful claws are soft and useless. Without a hiding place and its shell, the crab

*This hermit crab seeks a more accommodating shell size.*

could easily dry out or be eaten by other animals. On rare occasions, especially if a crab molts without burying itself, it might be eaten by other crabs. Because of this risk, some pet owners move their molting crabs to another cage, but this is usually unnecessary if the crab has buried itself.

Wait to remove the crab's old exoskeleton. Once its new exoskeleton hardens, the crab sometimes eats its old, empty exoskeleton, especially the thinner abdominal portion. After molting, a hermit crab does not necessarily need to find a new shell, but larger shells should be available.

If you are observant, you can often tell when your pet is getting ready to molt. A crab will become less active, often sit in one place, and not eat. Sometimes, the covering over the crab's eyes appears cloudy. Land hermit crabs continue to molt and grow throughout their lives. Young crabs molt more often than older ones. When a hermit crab is young, it can molt several times a year. As it gets older, it might only molt once every 12 to 18 months.

Once your pet has buried itself, try to resist the urge to see how your crab is progressing. Molting crabs should not be disturbed because you could accidentally hurt your pet, which is very soft at this time. If you are worried about your crab's welfare, wait until at least four weeks have passed before satisfying your curiosity. Then, if you must, gently dig away the sand or gravel from the crab. If your crab

is still alive, cover it and leave it alone. Keep in mind that interrupting your molting crab might cause it to come to the surface before it is ready. Pale and soft, your crab might dry out and die, or it might end up as a snack for your other crabs.

## Autotomy

Just like a lizard can lose its tail, a crab can lose its legs or claws, a process called autotomy. The break point for the crab's legs is located at the base of each joint. If the leg or claw is grabbed, it will break off. Muscular contraction at the joint closes it off and prevents a crab from bleeding. A molting hermit crab regenerates missing legs. After the first molt, the limb will be a small nub. It will take several molts, but eventually the appendage will grow back to its original size. However, if your hermit crab loses an eye, it will not necessarily regenerate the eye. Many crabs regrow a useless appendage in the place of their eye.

*Marine hermit crabs live in a variety of shells. This species* (**Trizopagurus strigatus**) *occupies a cone shell.*

In other species of crabs, the loss of an appendage is known to cause the crab to undergo a molt sooner than it otherwise would. Although it is possible, whether this occurs in land crabs is not definitively known by scientific studies or experiments.

# A Mobile Home

A land hermit crab selects a shell based on certain traits such as size, weight, size of the opening, and interior space. Crabs use the shells of several dozen species of marine snails for their homes. Although size is the most important consideration, the crabs also prefer the shells of certain species of marine snails. While wandering far from the ocean in mountains more than 2,000 feet (609 m) high, one hermit crab species will exchange their marine shells for the shells of land snails. If a shell is not available, a resourceful crab will tuck its abdomen into other items, such as pieces of coconut, and even garbage that washes ashore, such as bottle caps.

## Shell Modification

Land hermit crabs modify the inside of their shells by removing the columella and some-times the shells' lip. Such shells have a larger entrance and are roomier. Modified shells allow crabs to grow larger without completely out-growing their shell homes. Unmodified shells have less interior volume and are slowly enlarged by the hermit crabs who live in them.

*This hermit crab uses its large purple claw to block the entrance to its shell.*

Some of the large shells are used over and over by hermit crabs. Because large modified shells are uncommon, they are valuable and stay in a crab population. As soon as a large crab leaves the shell or dies, another crab immediately finds the shell and crawls into it. Through wear and long-term use, populations of land crabs create large numbers of modified shells.

# A Protective Home

Shells protect hermit crabs from predators and help prevent crabs from losing water and drying out. How well the crab fits into its shell is important. Well-fitting shells provide better protection from predators and allow the crabs to travel farther away from the ocean.

By necessity, hermit crabs often occupy shells that are smaller or larger than the size

they prefer. If land hermit crabs have a shell of the right size and shape, they are able to withdraw completely into the shell and block the opening of the shell with their left claw. If the crab cannot retract fully into its shell, it could be more susceptible to predators. A shell that is too large takes more energy for a small crab to carry around and might even slow the crab's walking speed.

Crabs try to avoid living in damaged shells. Just as you might not like shells with chips, cracks, holes, or pits, neither do crabs— although for different reasons. Damaged shells provide poor protection from physical stress, such as desiccation. Crabs in damaged shells try to exchange them for undamaged ones as soon as they can. Land hermit crabs quickly select and inhabit less damaged shells. If hermit crabs do not find the shells, they are washed away again by waves or buried in the sand.

# A New Home

Both wild and pet hermit crabs approach and investigate empty shells. When a crab spies a shell, it hurries over to inspect it. Grasping the shell with its claws and legs, the crab inserts a claw in the opening to assess the shell. After a careful examination, the crab decides whether to move into the shell.

Aligning the new shell with its current home, the crab holds onto both shells. Moving with great speed, the crab climbs into the new shell. Once inside, the shell might still prove unsatisfactory. Then the crab will return to its old shell.

## Shell Exchanges

Land hermit crabs locate potential new shells by detecting the smells from dead marine snails or from injured or dead hermit crabs. Such scents often attract numerous hermit crabs looking for new shells and large gatherings often form around the dead crab or snail. At such scenes, there is sometimes a mass exchange of shells. After one crab switches into the available shell, its old shell is free. A cascade of shell exchanges follows as the crabs swap up or down in size for better-fitting shells.

## Shell Competition

Wild hermit crabs have a continual housing problem. As they grow, they need new and larger shells. Although a crab might currently live in an ideal-fitting shell, eventually the shell will become snug and then the crab will need to look for a new one. However, wherever hermit crabs live, there are few empty shells. Most are already occupied by other crabs.

**Fighting.** A hermit crab in the market for a new shell might be lucky and find an unoccupied shell of the right size before another crab, or it might fight another crab for its shell. Fighting consists of a ritualized set of behaviors by which one crab forces another to switch shells. Marine hermit crabs are known to frequently fight and compete for shells. However,

*A land hermit crab investigates an empty snail shell.*

*A land hermit crab fills its shell with water.*

fights are much less common among wild and pet land hermit crabs (described in the section on aggression, see page 50).

## Shell Water

Land hermit crabs have a problem that aquatic hermit crabs do not; they need to find water. In their natural environment, most species of land hermit crabs store water in their shells (shell water). Large amounts of stored water allow hermit crabs to survive better in dry inland habitats away from the ocean. The water helps the crab keep its gills and branchial chamber moist, and makes breathing easier. Shell water plays an important role in the crab's osmoregulation, the control of water balance.

When a hermit crab fills its shell with water, it

**1.** places the tips of both claws together in its water dish;

**2.** makes shoveling movements with its claws, which have setae on their innerside, so

that capillary water rises toward its mouth (similar to a straw);

**3.** uses its maxillipeds to bring the water up to its mouth and the water flows into its branchial cavity;

**4.** raises the rear edge of its carapace and the water runs backward.

Vigorous pulsating movements of the abdomen help move the water so that it fills the space between the shell and the abdomen. The water also flows into the empty space in the shell behind the crab.

The water is kept in place by capillary action, a phenomenon whereby water molecules strongly adhere and cling to each other. In addition, the skin of the anterior part of the crab's abdomen is pressed firmly against the inner wall of the shell to prevent spilling.

Although a crab's shell is sometimes full of water, the crab can walk around without spilling any. However, when a crab is frightened and quickly withdraws deep into its shell, a large portion of the water can seep out.

# BUYING HERMIT CRABS

## How Many?

The hermit crab is not a hermit. Although a hermit crab can be kept by itself, ideally you should buy more than one. They are social animals that do best in groups, where they are more likely to be active and you are more likely to see their interesting behavior.

## Trinket or Long-Term Pet?

Most pet stores sell hermit crabs or can special order them for you. However, some pet owners obtain their crabs in more unusual ways: Sometimes the crabs are given away as prizes at carnivals and fairs, and sometimes people receive them as gag gifts from a sender who wants to make a statement about the recipient being "crabby."

Because of their low price and how they are sometimes displayed (on a pet store counter in a goldfish bowl), hermit crabs are often an impulse buy. Pets such as rabbits and parakeets are held in higher esteem than crabs, which are often considered disposable pets.

Hermit crabs have occasionally been subject to fads that attract media hype and attention. The shells that hermit crabs are sold in can contribute to such trends. Some crabs are sold in gold-edged shells. Crabs are also available in shells with various items attached, such as miniature football helmets or faux gemstones.

*It is a good idea to buy more than one hermit crab because they live best in groups.*

## Life Span

However you acquire your pets, it is important to remember that they are living animals and deserve proper, humane care. Hermit crabs are hardy, undemanding pets. Even those that are poorly cared for and neglected often live for 6 to 12 months. They can tolerate a lot of neglect, but they are also a potentially long-lived pet. Crabs that are well cared for can live in captivity for 6 to 15 years. There are anecdotal stories of crabs living up to 30 years in captivity. They are also rumored to live 50 to 70 years in the wild; however, these reports are unsubstantiated.

## Choosing a Crab

A healthy crab should be active. Because hermit crabs are awake at night, you might not have many active crabs to choose from when shopping during the day. Try to select a crab that is willing to come out of its shell when you pick it up or when you place it on the taut palm of your hand. At the very least, you should feel some slight movement from the crab inside its shell. If an active crab is in an unattractive shell, you can always provide it with more colorful shells for when it molts. Keep in mind that a crab becomes less active before it molts.

Pick up several crabs to get an idea of how they feel. Your choice should feel at least as heavy as other similar-sized crabs in the same types of shells. A crab that seems to weigh less when compared to the others might not be as healthy.

A crab is more likely to be healthy and less stressed if it lives in a shell that is not damaged and is not too small. Besides its claws and two pairs of walking legs, if you can see the crab's fourth pair of legs, its shell is far too small. The crab you select should not have any holes, pits, or abrasions on its body. You should be able to tell what is normal by observing and comparing it with the other crabs that are for sale. Although crabs can regenerate missing appendages, your first choice should be one with all its legs.

Avoid buying your crab from a crowded terrarium that is dirty and smells bad. The crabs are more likely to be unhealthy and the terrarium is more likely to be infested with flies and possibly mites. Although a rare occurrence, you should not see any mites walking on the crabs or in their home. Choosing a crab from a crowded cage is fine as long as the cage is clean.

Because crabs need a warm, humid environment, it is preferable to buy your hermit crab from a pet store that keeps them in a heated terrarium rather than in an unheated goldfish bowl or wire-frame cage. It is more difficult to maintain warm, humid conditions in such cages. Unless the pet store is warm and humid, the crabs might be stressed from not living in the required environment. Your choice of crabs might be reduced during the summer months because the crabs are often not imported during their breeding season.

## Which Size?

Hermit crabs are available in a range of sizes, from small dime-sized individuals to those the size of a baseball. Medium-sized crabs, about the size of golf balls, are available most often. Although crabs the size of dimes are cute, they tend to be more delicate and less forgiving of

*Land hermit crabs are social animals.*

*An active crab should be healthy.*

*Land hermit crabs are cute.*

variations in housing regime. They are a good choice for experienced hermit crab owners or people who are willing to more closely monitor the conditions of their small crab's home. Because they are not as hardy as larger crabs, many pet stores do not offer them for sale as often as the medium-sized crabs. Medium crabs measuring about 2 inches (5 cm) are a good size to start with because they are hardy and vigorous.

Very large crabs (jumbos) are sometimes available. Their size appeals to many people and makes them easy to watch. The larger the crab, the more expensive it will be. Jumbos can cost up to five times as much as medium-sized crabs. Be aware that jumbo crabs are proficient at locating molting cagemates and sometimes eating them. Small crabs are generally more active than large ones.

There are no hard and fast rules about the sizes of the crabs you keep together in a group. Some owners are successful at mixing together many sizes of crabs. However, there is always an increased chance that the large crabs will eat the small ones, especially after the small ones have molted. Also, small crabs are sometimes intimidated by larger ones and will become inactive. It is less risky to keep a group of same-sized crabs together.

# Extra Shells

Part of keeping land hermit crabs entails buying extra shells for them. Pet stores sell a variety of spare shells for hermit crabs that are imported from all over the world. Some shells are natural colored, some are gaudily painted in brilliant neon colors, and other shells are painted so that they glow in the dark. There are even shells decorated with glued-on baubles or some that have words painted on them. More sophisticated and expensive shells feature intricate hand-carvings from India. Most pet owners like the more dazzling colored shells compared to the natural ones.

Each of your hermit crabs should be provided with an assortment of two to three extra shells. The shell openings should be about ¼ inch (6 mm) larger than the shell in which a crab currently lives. You might select a shell for your crab because of its pretty color or shape, but your crab is more concerned with the shell's fit. A pet crab will be in the market for a new shell if it cannot retract its legs all the way into its shell.

*Because larger crabs have larger, more apparent claws, you are less likely to be pinched than by a small-size crab with small claws that are not as noticeable.*

Compared to the shells found in their natural environment, the shells sold at pet stores are shiny and almost always in good condition with no cracks or holes. In the wild, the shells that land hermit crabs live in are not nearly as attractive as those available for pets. A hermit crab living in a dull, inconspicuous shell is less likely to draw the attention of predators compared to a crab in a bright, colorful shell.

Some pet owners buy extra shells for their crabs at gift and craft stores. As long as the shells are not treated with potentially poisonous substances, such as glue that a crab could eat, they are usually safe for hermit crabs. Only select shells with a round opening. Hermit crabs cannot live in shells with a long narrow opening (such as the openings of conch shells).

## Which Species?

The purple claw crab is the species most commonly available. It is a colorful crab, usually different shades of red, in addition to its large purple or deep-red claw. Compared to the Ecuadorian crab, the purple claw is hardier and easier to care for because it is more tolerant of varying environmental conditions. However, some purple claws tend to be ornery, and until they are tame they might more readily pinch you.

The purple claw crab is the species sold as jumbos in pet stores. Many big crabs can weigh about ¼ pound (113 g). Their claws are very powerful and can break a pencil.

Compared to the purple claw, the Ecuadorian crab is small. When full grown, it weighs only about 1 ounce (28 g). Some are rather plain

*This is a marine hermit crab from the Florida Keys.*

colored, mottled with browns, grays, and whites, while others are tones of blue. Considered sweet and trusting, an Ecuadorian crab will hold your finger between its legs and nibble honey off it.

The care of both species is generally the same and these crabs can be housed together. However, the Ecuadorian crab has more difficulty molting in captivity than the purple claw and is less tolerant of poor housing conditions.

## Your Crab's Age

In general, large crabs are older than small crabs. The only way you can accurately estimate your crab's age is if it dies. Then the otoliths, small concretions of mineral deposits that sit atop the crab's balance organ (located at the base of each antennule), would need to be removed. The otoliths can be sectioned and the number of growth rings counted.

# HERMIT CRABS AS PETS

Hermit crabs are popular pets because they are inexpensive, hardy, and cute. They are relatively easy to care for when properly housed. These small animals can make good first pets for children who are properly supervised. They are a good choice for anyone who wants a low-maintenance pet, including elderly people, apartment dwellers, or people who want the pleasure of caring for an animal but do not have much time for a more demanding pet. Hermit crabs can be left without any special care while you go away for a long weekend.

Even though they are not cuddly pets, hermit crabs are personable enough that most pet owners give their crabs names and become quite fond of them. Hermit crabs have different personalities. Some are bold and curious. These fearless crabs quickly come out of their shells and crawl around on your hand. Others are shy. They hide in their shells and it is difficult to coax them out. It is exciting when you feel your crab's first tentative wiggle as it comes out of its shell and then see its maze of legs and antennae as it begins to walk around. When a crab feels threatened, it will quickly retract into its shell. Crabs are sensitive to movement. Until your pet is used to you, slow movements will be less likely to frighten your crab back into its shell.

*Hermit crabs are sold in a range of sizes.*

## Nocturnal Activity

Although some crabs might trundle around during the day, they are mostly nocturnal. The first part of the night is when your crabs will be most active. As pets, and in their natural habitat, hermit crabs are least active around noon. Many pet owners think that their crabs are boring because they do not do much. What many people do not realize is that their crabs are busiest while they are asleep. In addition, without adequate humidity and temperature, your pets will be less active.

Hermit crabs are relatively quiet. However, at night you might hear your crabs clank their shells against the terrarium walls or hear an occasional thud if one falls while climbing. Besides drinking and eating, your crabs might slowly walk the perimeter of their cage or burrow into the substrate. Using their walking legs and claws, they shovel the sand behind themselves and settle into the depression they make. Sometimes a crab will burrow along the glass sides of the terrarium. In the morning, you might see a crab peering out at you from several inches below the substrate surface.

## Handling Your Crabs

Crabs do not bite, but they can pinch. Even the small ones can break the skin and draw blood. Naturally, large crabs are capable of pinching even harder. Therefore, you must be careful when handling your pets. Never scoop

a crab up in the palm of your hand or you will most likely get pinched, even by a crab that is tame. To avoid being accidentally pinched, always pick up your crab from the back or top of its shell.

Many species of crabs are aggressive and will respond to your overtures with a threatening display. Waving their claws in the air, they will not hesitate to pinch if you try to pick them up. However, few hermit crabs try to pinch, which is one reason why they make nice pets. Either claw of a land hermit crab can be used to pinch. If you are pinched, it can hurt, especially if the crab will not let go. If this happens,

*Different sizes of crabs will need different sizes of shells.*

try to resist the reflexive urge to fling your crab to the floor. Instead, hold the crab under warm running water. If the crab still will not release its hold, use cold running water.

Hermit crabs are not pets that like to be played with or held. However, you can take them out of their cage. You can hold small crabs in your hand as long as you keep your hand flat and taut so the crab cannot accidentally pinch any loose skin. Sometimes it might feel like your hermit crab is pinching you with its claws. Because crabs use their pincers for climbing, your crab is probably just holding on so it can move and not fall. Your crab's walking legs end in pointy tips, which can feel sharp on your skin. Do not hold your crab in precarious positions. If it falls, it might die or lose one or more of its

*Pick up your hermit crab from the top or back of its shell.*

*Make sure you supervise your hermit crabs if you remove them from the safety of their cage.*

appendages. Many tame crabs will learn to eat their favorite foods while sitting on your hand.

Curiosity kills the crab. *Never try to pull your crab out of its shell.* For such small animals, they are amazingly strong and you will sooner tear your pet in half than extract it from its shell. Moreover, after such an experience, your crab is likely to quickly retreat inside its shell whenever you are near. When dead, a crab loosens its grip on the shell. When you pick up a dead crab, it will often fall out of its shell.

## Hazards

Many pet owners enjoy taking their pets outside their cage for some exercise. Your crab might enjoy wandering among your papers, exploring alongside walls, and even climbing up the curtains. Be careful when letting your crab explore outside its home. The pointy toes of their walking legs might get snagged in some types of carpet or fabric. If the crab struggles, it might break off a leg. It is best to let your crab walk around on smooth floors.

Although they are agile climbers, hermit crabs are also clumsy. In the wild, they fall out of the trees in which they climb and as pets they can tumble off tables, beds, or other high places. You can allow your pet crab to roam the floor or wherever you want as long as you are there to supervise it.

Do not allow your crabs to visit with other family pets. Besides the possibility of the other animal getting pinched, the crab might become a meal. Some large birds, such as parrots, might think the crabs are an interesting new toy and snatch them out of their shells. Animals such as pet rats can also attack your crabs.

Be cautious when sharing your pets with other people. Show your friends how to hold your crabs so they do not get pinched and your crab is not accidentally hurt.

# SETTING UP THE CAGE

## Cage Types

Because hermit crabs are inexpensive to buy, many people think that their pets' home should also be inexpensive. However, to properly care for hermit crabs, with the expectation that they will live for more than three to six months, they must be properly housed. Proper housing is a one-time expense that can help contribute to your pets' longevity.

Although a variety of cages can be used to house your hermit crabs, some types are better than others. The best type of housing for your crabs is a glass aquarium (to be used as a terrarium); the second best type is the hard plastic "critter cage" sold in most pet stores. Aquariums provide adequate room for your pets, and the internal environment (temperature and humidity) can be readily monitored and controlled. Because hermit crabs crawl on the ground and climb, either a standard or long aquarium is suitable.

Glass goldfish bowls are a poor choice because they provide a limited amount of space for your pets to crawl around and are more difficult to adequately heat and humidify. Hermit crabs are hardy animals and can survive for several months without showing any ill effects from improper housing. So while it might seem like your crabs can live in a goldfish bowl, ultimately they will need a more sophisticated setup if they are to survive and thrive.

*It is important to provide your hermit crabs with the proper cage substrate.*

Wire-frame cages of any style are not recommended. It is too difficult to regulate the temperature and humidity of such cages. In addition, hermit crabs could escape from such enclosures if they are constructed of vertical wire bars, such as a bird cage. Hermit crabs have been known to crawl out of their shells and squeeze out between the cage bars. Such adventures inevitably lead to a crab's death. Other types of containers constructed of wood and wire are not suitable for hermit crabs. The humid atmosphere the crabs require will rot the wood. Generally, the containers sold for breeding reptiles and invertebrates, such as tarantulas, are not suitable for hermit crabs because they are too small.

## Cage Size

The more crabs you keep, the bigger their enclosure should be. Hermit crabs are happiest living and climbing in a clean, roomy terrarium. It is most economical to buy a 10-gallon (40-L) aquarium rather than one of a smaller size. This size will provide enough room for three to five medium-sized crabs. Although you can keep more crabs in a 10-gallon (40-L) aquarium, the cage will get dirtier more quickly and need to be cleaned more often. Hard plastic cages are typically available in a wide range of sizes. The minimum size to buy is a 5-gallon (20-L) aquarium. Although you might be able to temporarily house your crabs in a smaller enclosure, they

will not survive as long. If you *must* house your crabs in a goldfish bowl, the minimum size to buy is the tall, 5-gallon (20-L) style.

*Usually, crabs of various sizes can be kept together safely.*

# Cage Placement

Do not place your pets' home near a heating or air-conditioning vent, in front of a window, or in a location that receives direct sunlight. Such conditions can rapidly heat or cool your crabs' home and might kill your pets. A hermit crab terrarium is not heavy and can be placed on a table, dresser, or desk. The floor is not a good location because temperatures tend to be more unstable. When nicely decorated, a hermit crab cage can be an attractive, intriguing part of a room.

# Temperature and Humidity

Land hermit crabs are tropical animals that need a warm, humid environment to thrive. The temperature in their home should be kept between 75–85°F (23.8–29.4°C). Hermit crabs are exotherms and their body temperature depends on the temperature of their surroundings. Your crabs will show little activity if the temperature is not high enough, even with a high relative humidity. When kept at temperatures below 65°F (18.3°C) for any length of time, they become inactive and lethargic. Just as their environment can be too cold, it can also be too hot. Temperatures over 90°F (32.2°C) should be avoided.

## Heating Methods

During part of the year, the natural temperature of some houses might be warmer than 70°F (21.1°C). However, it is unlikely that the ambient temperature of most homes is warm enough to support hermit crabs. At night, the temperature inside your house might also drop below the minimum needed by the crabs. Therefore, you will need to purchase an additional heat source to warm your pets' home.

There are several methods that you can use to heat the interior of your crabs' home. The best method is small, under-tank heating pads, which are made by several manufacturers. The pads are usually placed underneath the outside bottom of the cage. The ideal type is one that allows you to adjust the pad's setting if the cage temperature registers too high or too low. Be sure that the heating pad is the right size for your pets' cage and, if applicable, safe to use with a plastic cage. Sometimes heating pads can make a goldfish bowl (or even a terrarium) too hot. Raising the cage slightly above the pad should allow air flow and solve this problem. "Hot rocks" designed for reptiles to bask on will not create enough heat to warm the air of your crabs' home.

## Lighting

Because hermit crabs are nocturnal, the natural lighting in your house is sufficient for them. They do not require special, full-spectrum lights that are similar to sunlight. If you choose to heat your pets' home with a lightbulb, use a black, red, or ceramic bulb (sold in the reptile section of pet stores). These bulbs give off heat, but no light. They come in a variety of watts. Be sure you buy one of the appropriate size for your crabs' home. (Do not buy a light for a 50-gallon [200-L] aquarium if you only have a 10-gallon [40-L] aquarium.) This heating system tends to decrease the humidity in your crabs' home if you are not vigilant. Whatever method you choose, be sure to use a thermometer inside your pets' cage to monitor the temperature.

## Humidity

Your hermit crabs need a humid environment. About 70 percent is ideal, but most crabs will do well if the humidity is kept between 50 and 60 percent. Crabs that are kept at high temperatures and high humidities are most likely to be active and therefore more engaging pets. Besides a thermometer, it is useful to keep a humidity gauge in your pets' cage. If the gauge registers below 50 percent, you will know that you must increase the humidity.

In the crabs' warm environment, a large dish of water will often produce sufficient humidity through evaporation as long as the terrarium is covered. If you rely on this method, you must see to it that the dish is always full. Some water dishes made for reptiles are designed to be used with an aquarium pump and air stone. Such systems are also effective at maintaining the terrarium's humidity.

**Lids.** In order to maintain the humidity, your pets' home must be covered with a solid lid. The lid will also prevent your crabs from escaping.

## TIP

### Misting the Cage

You can also mist your crabs and their home with a plant mister filled with lukewarm water. Doing so will keep the terrarium humid and will cause your crabs to become very active. The heat will cause the water to evaporate and make the air humid. Using distilled water will prevent hard water stains from forming on the glass walls of your pets' home.

*Hermit crabs of all sizes need to climb.*

The folding glass cover that comes with an aquarium can be used for this purpose. However, do not cut any holes in the plastic strip attached to the glass cover. If your crabs are housed in a plastic cage with a vented lid, you will need to block many of the vents in the lid or the humidity will not remain high enough. Plastic wrap can be placed over the vents as long as no heat source is near the lid. You can regulate the cage's humidity and heat by keeping the cover partially open to allow some airflow. This means your pets' terrarium must also be covered with a wire screen so they cannot climb out and escape.

# Substrate

The best substrate to use in hermit crab cages is subject to considerable debate. Two of the best substrates are aquarium gravel sold for fish and high-quality sand. Use small, round gravel, not gravel with sharp edges. Round gravel is less likely to scrape your crab's exoskeleton. Sharp gravel could get inside your crab's shell and injure its soft abdomen and other parts of its body. The cut and abraded cuticle could get infected from bacteria and fungus.

## Sand

Some types of sand manufactured for use with reptiles can be used with your hermit crabs. If a pet store does not sell sand, it can be purchased at a hardware store. The sand sold for use in children's sandboxes is less coarse and of better quality than that sold to mix with cement. Be sure to wash, rinse, and air dry the sand before using it in your pets' home.

Some people who live near the ocean collect sand to use in their pets' home. This is fine as long as the sand is cleaned of debris. The trace minerals are believed to be beneficial to the crabs. Make sure that it is legal to collect the sand. In some locations, such as state parks, it might not be allowed.

## Soil and Other Materials

Sterilized potting soil sold for houseplants (without any plant enhancers that could be toxic to crabs) can also be used in your pets' home. Other materials sold for use with reptiles, such as moss and blocks of compressed, chopped vegetation (often coconut fibers), can be placed over the cage substrate. However, they should not be used as the sole floor covering.

## Burrowing

Pet hermit crabs burrow, often all the way to the bottom of the cage. The substrate caves in behind them as they tunnel. They do build a chamber at the end of their tunnel and ideally the substrate allows this rather than collapsing all about them. You need to provide your pets with enough substrate to completely cover themselves with several inches of the material. This means if you have a jumbo crab, you might need 7 to 10 inches (18–25 cm) of substrate in the cage. If you have small to medium crabs, place at least 4 to 5 inches (10–13 cm) on the floor of your pets' terrarium; 1 to 2 inches (2.5–5 cm) is not enough. In particular, the Ecuadorian crabs need a deep substrate to successfully molt.

Because hermit crabs like to dig, do not use reptile cage carpet. Nor should you use bedding made for small animals, such as shavings (especially cedar, which is used as a repellent for arthropods), corn cob, and recycled paper products. These products are designed to be absorbent and are inappropriate for a hermit crab's humid environment because they will quickly grow moldy.

# Interior Decoration

Crabs of all sizes need to climb, so include branches and rocks in their home. Pet stores sell
✔ rocks,
✔ driftwood,
✔ cholla wood,
✔ plastic replicas of logs with hiding places,
✔ and numerous other items that you can use in your crabs' cage.

You can also decorate with pieces of coral and shells, available in pet stores that sell marine fish.

Because crabs are nocturnal, arrange some of the items to provide some shady areas for them so that they can avoid the light. For example, a ceramic flower pot split in half and partially buried in the substrate will be used as a cave by your crabs, but still allows you to view your pets.

Crabs do not tend to rearrange their home, so you can put an item in the cage and it is unlikely to be knocked over or moved. Nonetheless, you can use aquarium silicone to glue any items to the back wall of the cage that could possibly fall and hurt your crabs. Some crab owners make a whole wall of coral and shells. This arrangement provides climbing and hiding places for the crabs.

Crabs will play on some kinds of toys sold for other pets. These include small mirrors (which a crab might dance around while looking at its reflection), plastic bird toys, and netlike hammocks sold for pet ferrets.

## Plants

Plastic plants sold for fish aquariums can add some bright color to your crabs' home, and some crabs will climb the plants. Compared to live plants, plastic plants are easy to keep and maintain in your pets' home. When dirty, they can be washed clean. However, hermit crabs do enjoy live plants. In particular, they like to shred them to pieces, occasionally taking a nibble. Some crab owners have noted that their pets will eat certain kinds of plants, but not others. It is generally assumed that if the plant is poisonous, the crabs will not eat it. However, there are more serious potential problems with live plants. Be aware that houseplants from nurseries often have toxic residues from pesticides, which can kill your crabs. The safest way to provide your crabs with live plants is to sprout the seeds in a wild bird mix. Grow the seeds in a small pot that you can easily take in and out of your crabs' cage. Your crabs will enjoy eating, digging, and destroying the plants. To contain the mess, you can place the pot on a piece of plain paper, which you can then remove.

As mentioned before, always cover your pets' home, not just to maintain the humidity, but because crabs are escape artists. Hermit crabs are capable climbers, even where it might appear there is little to grip. With the depth of substrate needed by some hermit crabs, it is obvious that your crabs' home must always be covered. Some crabs are strong and can push off a flimsy cover; therefore, you might need to place some weight on the lid.

When given a choice of land, freshwater, or seawater, land hermit crabs spend about 90 percent of their time on land. Therefore, you do not need to keep your pets in a terrarium with half water and half land because the crabs will rarely use the section with water. However, small, prefabricated waterfalls designed for reptile and amphibian cages can be used in hermit crab terrariums that are large enough. The waterfalls provide a good source of drinking water and humidity, and they make your pets' home more interesting.

## Cleaning the Cage

Your crabs' droppings will typically be hard and dry. They look like tiny pellets and do not usually smell. However, hermit crab owners often complain that an odor comes from their pets' cage. Most often, this smell is the result of feeding too much food and allowing uneaten food to remain in the cage. To combat this problem, reduce the amount fed and feed less pungent foods.

Tidy your pets' terrarium about once a week. If needed, rinse and dry the accessories and the food and water dishes. Look through the substrate and remove stored food and any visible droppings. Fungus and bacteria can grow in the warm, humid environment of your crabs' home. Every three to six months, you should

*Hermit crabs enjoy hiding in hollow logs and tunnels.*

replace the entire substrate, sooner if there is a persistent odor. (Be careful—some people who own numerous hermit crabs have accidentally dumped one of their pets when it was buried and molting!) Even if the substrate does not look dirty, it should still be changed. It is usually less time consuming and more convenient to buy new material rather than washing and drying the old substrate. If you use soap or bleach to clean your pets' home, be sure to thoroughly rinse and dry the cage before replacing your pets.

# FEEDING HERMIT CRABS

## What Wild Crabs Eat

Land hermit crabs are omnivorous scavengers. Omnivores are animals that eat both plant and animal foods. Scavengers eat whatever kinds of food they can find. In their native habitat, land hermit crabs eat a variety of items, including

✔ fruits,
✔ berries,
✔ seeds,
✔ plants,
✔ insects,
✔ fungi,
✔ feces,
✔ dead plants and animals,
✔ and agricultural crops such as plantain and rice.

Hermit crabs are not picky eaters. They take advantage of any available food. For example, the ocean's tide brings in items such as fruits and seeds, which the crabs will eat. However, any foods on the beach may be washed away during the next tidal cycle.

Some of the foods that wild hermit crabs eat are only available during certain times of the year. During the dry season, the spiny cedar trees that grow along the beaches flower. When the flowers of the blooming trees fall to the ground, large numbers of crabs gather beneath the trees and feast on the fallen blossoms. Every morning, the crabs eat the shed flowers until the trees are through flowering.

*Hermit crabs eat a wide variety of food.*

## Scavengers in the Wild

More specifically, hermit crabs eat the leaves and fruits of mangroves, coconuts, and tender, newly sprouted plants. Large numbers of hermit crabs cluster under fruit trees in orchards and feast on the ripe, fallen fruit. The crabs eagerly eat all kinds of wild fruit. They even eat the cactus fruits or "apples" of the manchineel tree, which are poisonous to most animals. In the dry season, the crabs eat the fleshy pads of opuntia cactus and gnaw on the trunks of certain types of trees. Scientists think that the crabs eat these latter two items for food and moisture. Hermit crabs also scavenge around people's homes and around garbage dumps. Island fishermen, who sometimes use the crabs as bait, lure the crabs into traps with coffee grounds. (The crabs themselves are not eaten by people.)

**Peculiar tastes.** In their natural environment, hermit crabs have voracious appetites for many things that we would find disgusting. For example, they are fond of fresh cow and horse manure, which they eat as a source of food and water. One species of *Coenobita* feasts on fresh tortoise droppings as quickly as the tortoises leave them. The crabs are also known to eat dog and human feces. (With the advent of modern plumbing on the islands where the crabs live, opportunities to consume the latter item have diminished. Nonetheless, when given the opportunity, the hermit crabs will eat all types of animal feces, including human.)

**Carrion.** Many types of carrion can occasionally be found on the beach, including dead fish, birds, crustaceans, and mammals. Hermit crabs find carrion very attractive and devour it with enthusiasm. In an incident recorded several decades ago, one scientist described how a dead donkey provided food for hundreds of crabs for weeks. Even when only an empty dried skin was left, the crabs still found the carcass irresistible. They climbed in and out of the donkey's carcass through numerous holes. The rattling sound of the crabs scuttling inside the carcass could be heard for a great distance.

**Detecting food.** Hermit crabs can locate potential food from a distance of more than 6 feet (1.8 m) through their senses of smell and vision. Certainly many of the items crabs eat have a pungent smell, such as dog and bird droppings, rotting bananas and fish, fresh and

*Wild hermit crabs feast on fallen fruit.*

overripe coconuts, fresh papaya, and ripe mangoes. Crabs can detect odors from these items at least 16 feet (4.9 m) away.

Hermit crabs are attracted to the sight of food and to each other. When a crab sees a cluster of feeding crabs, it will join the group. Large aggregations can form as more crabs gather on the food item. Scientists call this trait *social facilitation of foraging* and think it could improve the land hermit crabs' ability to locate food from a distance. When more than one crab is eating the same food item, the crabs tend to eat more quickly. Like grazing cows, most of the time the crabs rarely bother one another while they are eating. However, sometimes a large crab will flick away a smaller crab with its first leg.

### A Varied Diet

Although they are scavengers, hermit crabs do not just eat anything. One study found that hermit crabs preferred to eat foods that they had not recently eaten. As a result, hermit crabs eat a wide variety of foods because they seek new types of food to eat. This behavior might help the crabs eat a more nutritionally balanced diet and limit their exposure to toxins. While this behavior was found in the Ecuadorian crab, it is likely that it occurs in the purple claw crab as well. You will find that your pet crabs are not fussy eaters. Pet hermit crabs like to try new foods and even eat items that are not good for them, such as greasy potato chips.

## Commercial Foods

You should use a commercial food as the basis for your pets' diet. Pet stores sell a variety of foods for hermit crabs, including cakes, meal, canned moist food (similar to canned dog food), and dry granules. Some food manufacturers recommend that you add water to their food before feeding it to your crabs. Commercial diets are usually a mixture of fish, fruits, and grains. The nutritional content of prepared foods can vary widely, from about 18 to almost 50 percent protein.

The nutritional requirements for hermit crabs are not well known. Much of what we know about hermit crabs' diets comes from scientists who have observed the crabs in their natural environment. Information typically becomes available when people try to breed their pets, because animals must be healthy and well-fed in order to reproduce. Because hermit crabs are unlikely to ever be bred in captivity, this route is unlikely to become a source of information on hermit crab nutrition. However, hermit crabs are

### TIP

**Cuttlebone**

You must also provide your crabs with a source of calcium. Cuttlebone, sold in the bird department of pet stores, is the easiest way to satisfy this need. You can also grind eggshells and place them in the water dish, but this is much messier. Hermit crabs seem to enjoy playing on and eating the cuttlebone.

hardy and vigorous animals. Pet owners have been able to keep their crabs alive for years without knowing their specific requirements for nutrients such as protein, fat, and carbohydrates.

Commercial manufacturers of hermit crab diets have an interest in providing the best available food for your pets. Some manufacturers conduct feeding trials and other research on their diets. The results of one company's feeding trials have helped to make their foods more palatable, or tasty, to the crabs. From their research, scientists are learning what the crabs' requirements are for various nutrients, such as calcium and phosphorous. As more research is conducted and more is learned about the crabs' nutritional requirements, commercial manufacturers are better able to provide for these needs in their formulated foods.

## How Much to Feed?

Your hermit crabs should always have food available, such as the commercial diet you choose to feed. If water must be added to the

food, or if you feed moist canned food, be sure to replace it every day. If you are worried about wasting food, reduce the amount that you feed. Some dry foods can be left for several days before they need to be replaced.

You will notice that hermit crabs eat very little food. Through your own experience, you will learn how much food to leave for your crabs in order to avoid wasting it. Any moist foods can quickly spoil and smell in the humid atmosphere of your pets' cage. Therefore, offer only a small amount of these foods at one time. You can always give your crabs more at a later time.

When crabs are molting they do not eat. Sometimes, for no apparent reason, a crab will not eat for several days. Crabs can safely go more than a week without eating if they are already healthy. However, if your pet stops eating, make sure that the physical conditions

*Pet stores sell food for hermit crabs.*

in its home, such as heat and humidity, are satisfactory.

## Proper Feeding

Always place your crabs' food in a dish. Whatever kind of dish you use, be sure to keep it clean. Because they are nocturnal, it is best to give your crabs fresh food and treats in the evening. Usually the smell of their food will arouse your pets from their daytime sleep. When your crabs approach their food, you will see them flick their antennas. If you have several crabs of many sizes, you might need to have more than one food dish. Large crabs are better at getting food than small ones, and might prevent small crabs from getting enough food.

You will quickly learn that your crabs like to play with their food. They tend to drag pieces of food away from the dish, eat a bit, and then abandon it. Returning to their food dish, they will cart away and scatter other food items. Sometimes, they even bury uneaten pieces of food under the gravel or wood in their cage. This natural activity has an unfortunate consequence, because uneaten food in your pets' humid home will begin to rot. You will be surprised at how quickly such food can become moldy and smelly. Although your crabs might carry off some food, keeping their food in a dish will help prevent your pets' home from becoming too dirty and smelly.

## Treats and Supplements

Because hermit crabs are scavengers, they willingly try many new foods; therefore, they are relatively easy to feed. One of the best ways to ensure that your crabs eat a nutritious diet is to feed as varied a diet as possible. You should supplement your hermit crabs' prepared diet with small pieces of fresh foods.

**1.** Hermit crabs love fresh fruits and vegetables.

**2.** They are especially fond of grapes, raisins, lettuce, and peanut butter.

**3.** Hermit crabs will also eat bread, crackers, cooked grains (such as rice), dry unsweetened cereal, oatmeal, and pasta (without the sauce).

You can also offer your hermit crabs live or dead insects. Some crabs chase down crickets, which can be purchased at pet stores, but are often unable to eat them until the crickets are

dead. Treats of chicken bones can also be offered as long as they are removed after one night so they do not spoil. Naturally, none of the treats you feed should be spicy or sugar-coated. Crabs do enjoy an occasional treat of lightly salted popcorn.

You will need to experiment with how much of a treat to feed. A general rule is to leave the fresh food in your pets' cage for only 15 minutes. You might find that your crabs have individual food preferences. For example, one crab might relish peanut butter, but another might not. If you feed a small treat and your crabs eat it right away, you might be tempted to feed more. It is better to feed another type of food instead; otherwise, your crab might cart off any excess and hide it somewhere in its home.

*Hermit crabs often cluster around a food source.*

# Drinking Water

Your crabs will obtain water with some of their food, such as fresh fruits, but they still must always have fresh drinking water available. The water should be treated with an aquarium product to remove the chlorine. Pet stores are usually aware of the water conditions and whether any additional treatment is needed for your area. It is best to change the water daily, but every few days is adequate. Put the water in a large shallow dish that measures no more than 2 inches (5 cm) deep and at least 5 inches (13 cm) across, even if you only have two or three crabs. A large dish will minimize the chance of your crabs running out of water, whether by drinking it or by evaporation.

Your crabs will not only drink the water, but will wander through the dish, refilling their shell-water supply. They will stand in the water and flush out their shell water and any dirt inside their shells. Therefore, you must be certain that your crabs can easily walk in and out of their water dish. A safe amount to fill the container is with water no deeper than half the shell height of your smallest crab. Having water deeper than your crab is never a good idea. Although they can walk around in the water, hermit crabs cannot swim. If they are unable to get out, your pets will eventually drown. Natural sea sponges, which are sold for hermit crabs, can be placed in your pets' water dish to help them climb in and out. A small branch or rock in the dish will also work. However, many crabs enjoy sitting on the sea sponge for hours at a time.

Pet stores sell a variety of suitable containers that you can use as a water dish, including nontoxic ceramic dishes, plastic dishes, and large clam shells. Dishes made for reptiles also work well because of their rough texture. The crabs can readily get a foothold and easily climb in and out of the dish. (You can also partially bury the water dish so that it is level with the terrarium substrate.) One type of container is not necessarily better than the other. It should be noted that using a shell for water will not provide measurable amounts of additional calcium for your crab. (In any case, a quality commercial food and a cuttlebone should provide sufficient calcium.)

Do not use a metal container to provide your crabs with water. Metal ions can leach into the water and eventually might sicken and kill your crabs. Metal ions are needed in small amounts by all living organisms; however, the amount that your crabs might receive from the container could be harmful.

Your crab will drink by daintily dipping the tips of its claws in the water. Most often a crab will use its small claw to lift water drops and pass them to its third maxillipeds, which pass the water into its mouth and gill cavity. The tufts of setae on the crab's claws and maxillipeds help the crab collect the water. Crabs can use many water sources, and you might notice that your pets drink the water droplets that collect when you mist them.

# Salt Water

In addition to fresh drinking water, provide your crabs with a drinking container of salt water. Offer the salt water to your crabs at least once a week. Salt water is essential for Ecuadorian crabs. In the wild, they regularly fill their shells with brackish water or seawater. Although purple claw crabs may drink the salt water infrequently, you should still provide it.

*Make sure that you provide your hermit crabs with water for drinking and for cleaning out their shells.*

Salt made for use in fish aquariums is preferable to table salt. You can buy a mix sold for marine aquariums at pet stores. Besides salt, these commercial products typically include trace elements naturally found in seawater that may be beneficial for hermit crabs. Many brands contain directions for mixing up

a small volume. Any excess can be frozen and thawed for later use.

**Salinity.** Land hermit crabs can discriminate between water of different salinities. The purple claw crab prefers drinking water of a rather low salinity, although water the same salinity as seawater is used. If your crabs seem to consistently ignore the dish of seawater, try reducing the salinity of the solution to one half to two thirds of the recommended amount for seawater.

# HERMIT CRAB BEHAVIOR

## Grooming

A healthy crab grooms itself. When your crab looks busy and thoughtful, it might be busy scrubbing itself clean inside its shell. All creatures get dirty and groom themselves, including land crabs. Sand, dirt, and other granular matter can scrape and wear down the thin membranes between a crab's joints, or get stuck inside the crab's shell. Your pet's eyes and other sensory organs do not work as well when they are dirty.

Except for the stubby fourth legs, your crab will use all of its legs to groom itself. You will see your crab scrub its walking legs and claws against each other in various combinations of twos or threes. Using its small claw, a crab picks clean the surface of its large claw.

A crab also uses its feeding appendages to groom itself, in particular the third maxillipeds. Vision is important for land hermit crabs, and they spend a lot of time grooming their eyestalks. Moving its eyestalks downward, the crab hooks its third maxillipeds over them and sweeps down like brushing hair. The antennules are groomed in a similar manner.

The crab's small fifth legs are very flexible. These legs scrub the crab's abdomen, the base of all the other legs, most of the carapace, and the branchial chamber. After slipping into a new shell, the crab might need to clean out

*Hermit crabs groom themselves while inside their shells.*

dirt and other debris, which can increase the shell's weight. The crab does this while inside the shell, using its fifth legs to clean the shell's interior. The small claw is also used by the crab to scrub inside the shell and around the shell's opening. The crab's fifth legs are cleaned by the third maxillipeds.

You will most likely see your pets groom themselves after you mist them or when they stand in their water dish. Besides cleaning out its shell, if the water is deep enough, a crab will wash its eyestalks by repeatedly dipping them into the water and will also tilt forward to submerge its carapace.

You do not need to bathe your crabs as long as they are provided with sufficient water to groom themselves. Your crabs regulate their own internal shell water, and bathing them can disrupt this process. Although it might not be harmful, neither is it necessary. Bathing your crabs should not be considered a replacement for always having water available in a humid environment.

## Vocalization

Land hermit crabs make a variety of sounds that have been described as whirring, croaking, and chirping. The sounds vary from a constant whir to bursts of the croaking-chirping sound. Sometimes called stridulations, the sounds can be heard from several feet away. It is thought that these sounds might be produced by the

crab wrapping its appendages together and rubbing and tapping them against the inside of its shell. If you pick up your hermit crab when it is producing these sounds, you might feel vibrations inside the shell.

Usually the sounds are only heard when crabs interact; they often accompany aggressive displays and shell fights. However, Ecuadorian crabs have been heard chirping when they were not noticeably interacting with one another. Male Ecuadorian crabs tend to chirp more often than females. These noises are seldom heard among pet crabs.

*This marine hermit crab uses its legs and claws to interact with other crabs.*

## Aggression

Hermit crabs more often communicate with each other by using their legs and claws. They casually climb over each other and even rest in piles atop one another. Sometimes when a crab approaches or passes by another crab a distance away, it will raise its leg.

On occasion, the crabs act more irritated with one another. Then they will slowly raise a walking leg or a claw. The crab will remain stiff like this for a few moments, or bring its legs back to the ground right away. Occasionally a crab raises its first leg up and toward the eye-stalk region of the other crab. It might strike the eye of the other crab or lower its leg back to the normal position without any contact.

Hermit crabs sometimes have pushing contests. The combatants push each other back and forth with their big claws while at the same time keeping one or more of their walking legs raised. Sometimes the threat of such force is enough to cause one crab to retreat without any physical contact. During these interactions,

*Sometimes hermit crabs will compete for shells.*

the crabs' antennas and antennules often wave up and down at varying speeds.

## Shell Fights

Shell fights occasionally occur among wild and pet hermit crabs and can often be detected because of chirping sounds. From a position slightly above the defending crab's shell, an attacking crab seizes the defending crab with its walking legs and rapidly rotates it back and forth. While doing this, the attacker's claws are usually inside the opening of the defending crab's shell. This shaking often drives the defending crab from the shell that the attacker wants. Practically leaping out of its shell, the loser waits and enters the victor's shell. Typically, neither crab is harmed and both might get a better-fitting shell.

# HERMIT CRAB REPRODUCTION

## Determining Gender

There are no visible external differences between female and male land hermit crabs. Although males typically grow larger than females, the sexes do not differ noticeably in color or other aspects of their external morphology. The features that distinguish females from males are only visible when the hermit crabs are completely outside their shells. Female crabs can be identified from the gonopores (the female's genital openings) on the first segment of their third legs. The gonopores look like tiny oval or circular holes. In addition, mature females have large, setae-covered pleopods on the left side of their abdomens. Male crabs do not have these features, but they do have papilla: tiny, pimplelike projections on their fifth legs.

The only time you might be able to tell the sex of your pet crab is if it dies (dead crabs often fall out of their shells) or when it molts. Although many crabs eat their molted exoskeleton and should be allowed to do so, the differences that distinguish the sexes are reproduced on the crab's exoskeleton. Thus, if the crab is a female, you ought to be able to see the gonopore openings on the base of her third legs.

As a pet owner, you need not be concerned with the gender of your pets. Because no one

*A crab's gender does not affect its looks or its behavior.*

else can tell what the sex of your crab is, it is perfectly fine to call a female Fred or a male Alice. Furthermore, because your crabs will not breed in captivity, their gender is not relevant, nor will their behavior as pets be affected by their gender.

## Mating

Little is known about reproduction in land hermit crabs. It is an area that has not received much scientific study. Most of the studies that have been done involve the purple claw crab. This crab breeds over several months during the summer and autumn. They migrate from their inland homes to their coastal breeding sites. This trip usually occurs several weeks out of the year. The crabs may walk several miles during their journey to the coast. This mass movement is probably responsible for the stories of hermit crabs traveling in packs. On some Caribbean Islands, people have reported seeing thousands of crabs descend gullies and climb slopes as they travel down established tracks to the coast. The hermit crabs tend to use the same paths year after year.

Mating occurs during migration to the sea. Usually crabs of similar sizes mate. The male crab initiates mating by grasping the opening of the female's shell and moving her shell from side to side. A series of rocking and tapping motions stimulates the female to extend from her shell. The crabs mate by extending their

*Hermit crab reproduction has received little study.*

bodies about three quarters of the way out of their shell so that the ventral portion of both their bodies can meet. Using his small legs, the male passes the spermatophore to the female. However, if the female is uninterested, she will retract into her shell. The male lets go of her shell and they do not mate.

# Eggs and Larvae

Some time after fertilization, the female hermit crab extrudes the eggs into her shell. She gathers and attaches the eggs to her pleopods and then broods them inside her shell. As the eggs develop within the female's shell, they are protected from predators and dehydration.

The female keeps her eggs clean by grooming them with her fourth and fifth legs, along with her small claw. Naturally, eggs brooded in damaged shells are not as well protected. Depending on the crab's size, female purple claw crabs may lay between 1,000 to 50,000 eggs. Larger females produce more eggs than do smaller females.

**1.** As the eggs develop, they change in color from dark reddish brown to pale blue or gray. After about three weeks, the eggs are ready to hatch.

**2.** At low tide, the female moves toward the sea, but does not enter the water. Using her fifth legs, she picks up small clusters of fully developed eggs from the egg mass attached to her pleopods.

**3.** She takes the eggs further out of her shell with her maxillipeds and claws. Then she drops or flings the eggs onto the wet rocks where they hatch when the ocean water washes over them.

## Zoeae

When the eggs hatch, the individuals do not look like hermit crabs. Hermit crabs, like other crustaceans, must first go through several larval stages of development before they become adults. The newly hatched hermit crab larvae are called zoeae. They measure about $\frac{1}{8}$ of an inch (3 mm) and are visible without a microscope. The zoeae have large bulging eyes and long shrimplike bodies. They spend most of their time swimming in the ocean as part of the plankton. Many of the zoeae are eaten by larger sea animals such as fish. While they are larvae, hermit crabs are carnivorous and feed on other tiny animals.

As larvae, hermit crabs drift on ocean currents. Sometimes they are dispersed to other areas from those in which they where initially hatched. In other cases, the ocean's eddies and currents keep them in the same island location.

## Glaucothoe

The zoeae grow and develop by molting through a number of stages. The number of stages varies with the species of crab. For the purple claw hermit crab, there are usually between four and five, although sometimes there are up to six. Each zoeal stage can last almost a week. At each molt, the zoeae grow larger and sometimes add more appendages. The zoeal larval development takes about 26 days, after which a transformation point is reached and the larvae molt to a postlarval stage called the glaucothoe or megalops. At this stage, the animal looks more like an adult hermit crab and both swims and walks about. After at least another month, the glaucothoe metamorphoses to become the juvenile land hermit crab.

While still living in the ocean, the glaucothoe begin to search for shells in which to live. Newly metamorphosed juvenile crabs can find their first shells underwater by detecting cues from dead snails. Tiny crabs that crawl ashore without shells will usually die. When the Ecuadorian crabs first come ashore, they are transparent and measure about $\frac{1}{5}$ of an inch (5 mm).

## Juvenile Crabs

The crabs then move to the land, where they mainly lead a nocturnal existence. During the day, they seek shelter in cracks under ledges or

*Marine and land hermit crabs do not breed in captivity.*

logs, or bury themselves in the sand. Sometimes they are active during the day, such as in humid conditions or in rain. After a few more molts, the little crabs can move further and further away from the ocean. Typically, purple claw hermit crabs are ready to breed by their second year. By this time, they have passed through a molt called the puberty molt, where the pleopods and other structures needed for reproduction are fully developed.

*A full-grown hermit crab.*

# Breeding in Captivity

Part of keeping animals as pets is the thrill and fascination that comes from being able to breed them. However, land hermit crabs are unlikely to ever be bred in captivity due to their specialized requirements, and there are currently no captive breeding programs. Even under laboratory conditions, they can be diffi-cult to rear. Many of the larvae do not survive to successfully metamorphose. Furthermore, there is little economic incentive to breed them because they sell for very little in pet stores.

Sometimes female crabs that have ripe eggs are imported during the summer. When the females are placed in an aquarium with access to seawater, a few hatchlings might be obtained. The zoeal larvae might develop if fed freshly hatched brine shrimp. However, usually the eggs are no longer viable due to the crabs' long trip.

Even though hermit crabs have been kept as pets for more than 20 years, little is known about any illnesses that might affect them. Some signs of a sick crab include lethargy, paralysis, refusal to eat, trembling legs, and unusual changes in the coloring of the exoskeleton, such as darkening or lightening.

Of course, some of these are also the symptoms of a crab before it molts. Pet crabs are sometimes unable to successfully molt. Remember, your crab needs a humid environment, otherwise it might have difficulty. In addition, the cage substrate must be deep enough for your largest crab to burrow several inches below the surface.

## Cage Pests

Many wild animals are naturally infested by a normal complement of mites, not all of which are bad. At least four species of mites are known to associate with the purple claw crab. One type spends its entire life among the crab's gills, but it is not believed to be detrimental because it does not damage the gills. Another species of mites uses the crabs to travel from place to place because they cannot move on their own. The mites climb aboard the crabs and ride until they are in the next appropriate habitat and then leave. These mites are of little concern to pet owners because they do not physically harm the crab. Furthermore, you are unlikely to ever see them and unlikely to ever get rid of them.

The situation is different if you notice mites in your crabs' terrarium. They are probably the result of a dirty environment or contamination from an outside source. To get rid of them, you will need to completely replace the cage substrate and any wooden items. Wash the aquarium and other items such as rocks in soapy water. Soaking your crabs for a few moments in lukewarm water will cause any mites sharing your crabs' shells to float to the water's surface. Dispose of them down a sink, not in the garbage. Commercial preparations made to kill mites on other pets are not recommended. Because crabs and mites are both arthropods, the product might also kill your crab.

On occasion, pet crabs kept in dirty cages with rotting food have been subject to fly infestations from both fruit flies and other species. The maggots from these flies have been found inside the crab's shell and are assumed to be detrimental.

*Not much is known about illnesses that affect hermit crabs.*

## Books

Burggren, W. W., and B. R. McMahon. *Biology of the Land Crabs.* Cambridge, England: Cambridge University Press, 1988.

Schram, F. R. *Crustacea.* Oxford, England: Oxford University Press, 1986.

Street, P. *The Crab and Its Relatives.* Plymouth, England: Latimer Trend & Co., 1966.

## Journal Article

Hazlett, B. "The Behavioral Ecology of Hermit Crabs." *Annual Review Ecology and Systematics,* volume 12, pages 1–22.

## Magazine

*Critters USA*
Fancy Publications Inc.
P.O. Box 6050
Mission Viejo, CA 92690
(949) 855-8822

## Manufacturers of Supplies

Florida Marine Research
1530 Mango Avenue
Sarasota, FL 34237
(941) 365-5753

Tetra/Second Nature
3001 Commerce Street
Blacksburg, VA 24060

Timberline
201 East Timberline Road
Marion, IL 62959
1-800-423-2248

T-Rex
1124 Bay Boulevard, Suite A
Chula Vista, CA 91911
Corporate office: (619) 424-1050

Zoo Med Laboratories, Inc.
3100 McMillan Road
San Luis Obispo, CA 93401
(805) 542-9988

## About the Author

Sue Fox is a consulting wildlife biologist and freelance writer. She worked in pet stores for more than ten years. She is the author of several books on small animals and is a regular contributor to *Pet Business* magazine. Her home in the Sierra Nevada Mountains of California is shared with a menagerie of invertebrate and vertebrate animals.

## Photo Credits

Isabelle Francais: pages 2, 3, 10, 31, 32, 40, 47, 48, 61; Mella Panzella: pages 30 (top), 42; Zig Leszczynski: front cover, inside front cover, inside back cover, back cover, pages 4, 6–9, 12–16, 18–22, 24–28, 30 (bottom), 34, 36, 39, 44, 45, 50–52, 54, 56–58

## Acknowledgments

The author would like to thank the following people and companies for sharing their expertise on hermit crabs: Dr. Renae Brodie, Don Drenning, Florida Marine Research, Dr. Sandra Gilchrist, Dr. Brian Hazlett, Linda Kogin, Dr. Barry O'Connor, Tetra/Second Nature, T-Rex, Quality Reptiles, and Zoo Med Laboratories; and special thanks to my patient editor, Lynne Vessie. Any errors are solely the responsibility of the author.

## Important Note

Although hermit crabs are not poisonous and do not bite, they do have strong claws. When you handle hermit crabs, you might sometimes get pinched. If a powerful pinch breaks the skin and signs of infection develop, see a physician immediately. No diseases are currently known that can be transmitted from hermit crabs to people. Nonetheless, preventive health measures are still advised. Always wash your hands before and after handling your hermit crabs.

*All inquiries should be addressed to:*
Barron's Educational Series, Inc.
250 Wireless Boulevard
Hauppauge, NY 11788
http://www.barronseduc.com

Library of Congress Catalog Card No. 99-042836

International Standard Book No. 0-7641-1229-5

**Library of Congress Cataloging-in-Publication Data**
Fox, Sue, 1962–
    Hermit crabs / Sue Fox.
        p.  cm. — (Complete pet owner's manual)
    ISBN 0-7641-1229-5 (pbk.)
    1. Hermit crabs as pets. I. Title. II. Series.
SF459.H47F69    2000
6399'.67—dc21                                99-042836
                                                      CIP

Printed in China